IT'S TIME TO LEARN ABOUT BORDER COLLIES

It's Time to Learn about Border Collies

Walter the Educator

Silent King Books
A WhichHead Entertainment Imprint

Copyright © 2025 by Walter the Educator

All rights reserved. No part of this book may be reproduced in any manner whatsoever without written per- mission except in the case of brief quotations embodied in critical articles and reviews.

First Printing, 2024

Disclaimer

This book is a literary work; the story is not about specific persons, locations, situations, and/or circumstances unless mentioned in a historical context. Any resemblance to real persons, locations, situations, and/or circumstances is coincidental. This book is for entertainment and informational purposes only. The author and publisher offer this information without warranties expressed or implied. No matter the grounds, neither the author nor the publisher will be accountable for any losses, injuries, or other damages caused by the reader's use of this book. The use of this book acknowledges an understanding and acceptance of this disclaimer.

It's Time to Learn about Border Collies is a collectible early learning book by Walter the Educator suitable for all ages belonging to Walter the Educator's Time to Eat Book Series. Collect more books at WaltertheEducator.com

USE THE EXTRA SPACE TO TAKE NOTES AND DOCUMENT YOUR MEMORIES

BORDER COLLIES

Out on the farm, so quick and bright,

It's Time to Learn about
Border Collies

A Border Collie runs with might.

With black and white or brown so neat,

It dashes fast on nimble feet!

Its eyes are sharp, so big and wide,

Watching sheep that run and hide.

It crouches low, then gives a stare,

To guide them back with skill and care.

So smart and quick, it knows the way,

To help its owner every day.

It learns so fast, it loves to try,

To fetch, to spin, to jump up high!

It runs in circles, left and right,

Moving sheep from day to night.

It doesn't bark, it moves with grace,

With steady steps, it keeps the pace.

It's Time to Learn about
Border Collies

A Border Collie loves to play,

It chases balls all through the day.

It jumps through hoops and weaves so tight,

A champion dog, so strong and light!

Its fur is soft, both short and long,

With wagging tail so proud and strong.

It loves the wind, it loves the air,

It loves to run just everywhere!

It's kind and sweet, but needs to move,

It wants to run, it wants to groove!

If left alone with time to spare,

It might just zoom from here to there!

With happy heart and working mind,

A Border Collie's one of a kind.

It learns new tricks, it helps with chores,

It's Time to Learn about
Border Collies

And always wants to learn some more!

A loyal friend, both brave and true,

It sticks with you the whole day through.

It snuggles close when work is done,

And rests until the morning sun.

So if you see this dog so bright,

Running fast from left to right,

Just know it loves to work and play,

It's Time to Learn about
Border Collies

A Border Collie leads the way!

ABOUT THE CREATOR

Walter the Educator is one of the pseudonyms for Walter Anderson. Formally educated in Chemistry, Business, and Education, he is an educator, an author, a diverse entrepreneur, and he is the son of a disabled war veteran. "Walter the Educator" shares his time between educating and creating. He holds interests and owns several creative projects that entertain, enlighten, enhance, and educate, hoping to inspire and motivate you. Follow, find new works, and stay up to date with Walter the Educator™

at WaltertheEducator.com

www.ingramcontent.com/pod-product-compliance
Lightning Source LLC
LaVergne TN
LVHW051919060526
838201LV00060B/4078